MIDNIGHT, DHAKA

For my father, Mir Mahboob Ali,
whose voice I always hear reciting poetry to me.

MIDNIGHT, DHAKA

Mir Mafhuz Ali

SEREN

Seren is the book imprint of
Poetry Wales Press Ltd.
57 Nolton Street, Bridgend, Wales, CF31 3AE
www.serenbooks.com
facebook.com/SerenBooks
twitter@SerenBooks

ISBN: 978-1-78172-159-9
e-book: 978-1-78172-160-5
Kindle: 978-1-78172- 161-2

A CIP record for this title is available from the British Library.

The publisher acknowledges the financial assistance of the Welsh Books Council.

Book Cover Design: Khandaker Enamul Haque
Artist: Aniruddha Kar

Printed in Bembo by Bell & Bain Ltd, Glasgow

Author website: www.mirmahfuzali.com

Contents

Midnight, Dhaka, 25 March 1971   7
My Salma   8
Hurricane   10
Our Boowah   12
Nandita   13
Cord   14
Jonaki   16
My First Shock at School   17
A Bengali Girl in a Shy Village   18
Billkiss   19
Baby Snatchers' Hill   20
Early Morning, Polished Boots   22
The Nectarine Tree   28
Flies   29
My Mistress Grounded Me   30
MIG-21 Raids at Shegontola   31
Illegitimate   32
An Open Manhole   34
Bangladesh   35
Boy in an Old Photograph   36
Skylark   37
A Basket of Sorrow   38
Bidisha on the Wall   40
Mind of a Stone   41
A Lizard by My Hospital Bed   42
Bullet   43
My Maestro   44
Dog Seed   45
When Bangladesh Floats in a Water-hyacinth   46
My Aim Now is to Waste Time Luxuriously   47
Suzanne   48
Why Doesn't My Sister Sing to Me Anymore?   49
To Have My Sister Back   50
She May be in the Summer Berries   52
Famine   53

My Father, a Disconnected Man   54
Still Birth   55
Mother to Son   56
My Child, Cycling   57
I Want to Change the Course of a Great River   58
An English Viper and Indian Cobra   59
My Son Waits by the Door   60
The Last Apple in a Bowl of Fruit   61

Acknowledgements   63
About the Author   64

Midnight, Dhaka, 25 March 1971

I am a hardened camera clicking at midnight.
I have caught it all – the screeching tanks
pounding the city under the massy heat,
searchlights dicing the streets like bayonets.
Kalashnikovs mowing down rickshaw pullers,
vendor sellers, beggars on the pavements.
I click on, despite the dry and bitter dust
scratched on the lake-black water of my Nikon eye,
at a Bedford truck waiting by the roadside,
at two soldiers holding the dead by their hands and legs,
throwing them into the back, hurling
them one upon another until the floor
is loaded to the sky's armpits. The corpses stare
at our star's succulent whiteness
with their arms flung out as if to bridge a nation.
Their bodies shake when the lorry chugs.
I click as the soldiers laugh at the billboard on the bulkhead:
GUINNESS IS GOOD FOR YOU
SIX MILLION DRUNK EVERY DAY.

My Salma

Forgive me badho, my camellia bush,
when you are full of yourself and blooming,

you may ask why, having spent so many years
comfortably in your breasts, I still dream of Salma's,

just as I did when I was a hungry boy in shorts,
her perfect fullness amongst chestnut leaves.

The long grass broke as I ran, leaving
its pollen on my bare legs.

When the soldiers came, even the wind
at my heels began to worship Salma's beauty.

★

A soldier kicked me in the ribs. I fell
to the ground wailing.

They brought Salma into the yard,
asked me to watch how they would explode

a bullet into her. But I turned my head away
as they ripped her begooni blouse,

exposing her startled flesh. The young soldier
held my head, twisting it back towards her,

urging me to spit at a woman
as I might spit a melon seed into the olive dirt.

★

The soldier decorated with two silver bars
and two half-inch stripes was the first to drop his

ironed khaki trousers and dive on top of Salma.
His back arched as she fought for the last leaf

of her dignity. He laughed as he pumped
his rifle-blue buttocks in the Hemonti sun.

Then covered in Bengal's soft soil, he offered
her to the next soldier in line.

They all had their share of her,
dragged her away out of the yard.

I went in search of Salma,
among the firewood in the jungle.

★

I stood in the middle of a boot-bruised field,
working out how the wind might lead me to her.

Then I saw against the deepening sky
a thin mangey bitch, tearing at a body with no head,

breasts cut off in a fine lament.
I knew then who she was, and kicked

the bitch in the ribs, the same way
that I had been booted in the chest.

Hurricane

A storm roared over the Bay of Bengal,
a glass bull, charging with its horns.
It pounded throughout the long night
as we children huddled together

inside our fatherless bungalow.
We watched our tin roof rip off.
First from its tie beams
then the ceiling joists. One by one

the rest of the house vanished
as we covered our heads with our hands
and saw our possessions take flight –
The Koran, War and Peace, Gitanjali,

the clothes in the alna, shoes and sandals,
sisters' dolls and brothers' cricket bats.
We children couldn't understand
what sins we'd committed,

but we asked God's forgiveness.
We thought the worst was over.
Then came the giant waves
one after the other snatching us

from the arms of our mother,
tossing us like cheap wood.
Trees fell, exposing their great roots.
Cats and cattle lay dead on the ground.

Our bodies shrivelled with water,
shuddered like old engines.
Teeth rattled to the point of rapture.
The sun came very late that day,

found us trapped in a wind-sheared tree.
We couldn't hear the birds singing
or the muezzin calling for prayer. Silence,
the new disease, swept across our land.

Our Boowah

Our housemaid
is a tiny woman
with a lanky grey body.
Her face is round,
eyes amber,
slight limbs are dark
and yet sweet like raisins.
She wears no lavender powder
or brightly-coloured lipstick
unless there is a party.

Her constant laughter
tells you she was once
a langur
who leapt
and made the tree tops
quiver
with her monkey wish.

This woman thinks
she is still
in the Garo Hills,
crouching behind
a lantana bush and free
to do whatever she likes
with us children.
This is the woman
who fed me bananas
and peanuts with her hand,
let me hang from her neck,
ride on her slim back.

She lulled me to sleep
with her strange songs,
tapped my back
and taught me
not to have nightmares.

Nandita

Someone could have told me
you have to rot before you ripen –
days of open fields
and running free, of ruining my shirt
by going into the sugar-canes
with the Hindu girl Nandita,
showing her the language of the bush
in the mist-flavoured twilight.
The lilt of her sari roused
the leaves we needed for our art.
A hot tincture in her blouse
drove me to be with her mouth.
At first, she turned me away
then she washed me
in that blue rustling hedge
while the country slid
inside her shitala quilt.
Many times we hid under the little candle
of the iced moon, senses tingling
to the last drop of dawn.

Cord

Ask the bimal bamboo
    that carries my name
in its long slender canes.
    It will tell you I belong
here among the jaruls and jamruls
    by the clay-pond banks
at the back of the house
    where I was born many harvests ago.

I am not a stranger
to the boatman, Kadam Ali,
or the village poet, Folo Bibi,
and her roaming ally, Bawool Srimathi.
        They might have told you
how I pierced the pitchers
on girls' heads with my sling shots,
        soaking their kortas and kamizes.
But you should have heard
how I played naked
in the monsoon mud
with Saima Nanda.

I am not a stranger
to the smell of the earth.
Many times I helped Jabor Ullah
plough the hard land
softened by morning mist.
I saw how he sniffed the odour
of the earth cradled in his hands,
pushed me to understand
the thick richness of cow dung.

I am not a stranger
to the willow's
melt through the water,
rippling the dinghy's sleep.
If you care to roll your eyes on
what I have done
before I began a runaway life.

I am not an outsider,
though I am travelling through this field,
and a river journeying through me,
is carrying the silt of every memory.
While I am thatching a roof
or building up a hay-sack.
My umbilical cord is buried
under that orange tree in June.

Jonaki

O firefly! You have come out
of the hedgebank shadow.
But your flickering flight
cannot drive back the dark.
You neither have the sun's fire
nor the moon's ice. Your white
lantern blinks on and off, wants
to sleep and dream the life of trees
which burrow their roots into the wet
to terrify the worms. If
the trees could babble, they'd
only hum some low green note
for the lonely place where
ripe fruits wake the birds.

My First Shock at School

Muktar was his name – his tongue
still white with his mother's milk –
and he sucked his thumb in the classroom.
Monsoon music drowned the day.
Our Lakeside School was surrounded by black waters.
Water-hyacinth, rice-grass and lotus covered the lake.
Tiffin time. Playground muddy.
We had nowhere to go at break, but watched
how the rain-mist dusted our eyes – a white darkness.
He led me to the back of our school.
We stood at the water's edge.
He took his fleshy shoot out of his pouch.
It was small as a young gherkin,
a yellow flower still attached to its head.
I laughed. He took my hand, pulled it
and asked me to touch, as if to take the flower
with the ant that hid in its pollen.
I snatched my hand away.
He wanted to slide mine out of my blue shorts,
measure it against his.
I refused. He insisted again,
said it was tiny and soft as a leech.
I reached out into the darkness of my pants.
His eyes sparked as if he'd just seen a spikenard bloom.

A Bengali Girl in a Shy Village

Why are you so shy, Ravenkoli?
You haven't lived long enough to know truth from a trick.
Your naked feet skim the earth.

Your birthplace tunes well with your skin.
Nobody seems to notice what you are – a Kak orchid.
I want to wear your flower's Bengali vowels around my neck

and put the grammar right
according to the rules in your village.
To others you may be just a black bud

unable to stand proud on your own stem
or ripple those petals
for their first shiver in the air

but I have seen your urgent body dance
from the blue cirrus wood
wrapped in the yellow sari of the sun.

Billkiss

She heard Nildeep's heavy shadow,
breaking the dry leaves on the heron-road
and like a cyclone she swirled for a redbud tree
to greet him where they first met in spring.
They hugged hard under the moving grass.
His city tongue rolling in her rural mouth,
bubbles popping her taut skin.
A great tongue, that smart boy almost
beat the throb out of her,
brought too much meaning into her life.
She did not know then a kiss is just
a foreign fruit she should always try
before a bee ploughs into its belly.
She only thought of how the two tongues moved,
how she was blacked-out in his kiss.
Snogging was better than sleep.
She was still dizzy when she promised:
"I'll never wash you off my lips."
The twelve-year-old Billkiss now
refused to eat or brush her teeth.
Her school mates declined to sit near her.

Baby Snatchers' Hill

Trees had a breeze on them. I was probably five. A fine cool day. We travelled on a minibus with my uncles and aunties, our destination, the Garo Hills, where the jungles were dark below the eastern Himalayas. We heard the Garoes were tiny black people, but their hearts were bright. They welcomed visitors with palm wine.

Night was charcoal. Silence was loud. Fireflies moved like shooting stars. We stopped for a rest, climbed out of the bus and loosened our muscles. I thought I heard a distant cry clear as a cricket chirp and grabbed my uncle Monsur's hand. He held me tight, hushed us all, asking us to listen to the sound coming from the depths of the forest. We stayed all together and followed the cry.

We heard it again at regular intervals. Our uncle Montu hadn't forgotten to take with him his double-barrel gun. The closer we went the clearer it was to us – the sound of a boy. A little distance away on a hill there was a thatched house long abandoned by its owner, its lattice walls falling apart, a hurricane light flicking its slow glare inside.

We poked through the house's many holes and discovered a boy of my age. Naked, tied to a beam with jute thicker than his arms. The man had a goat-beard, wore a long garment, a round white topi on his head. He was more like a madrassa teacher than a monk.

He had a stout stick the size of a baseball bat in his right hand. Kept hitting the boy who had more bones than flesh. My eyes roved around the large room. The house was full of stretchers, walking sticks, pushchairs made with the wheels of children's prams. In another room a set of ten makeshift beds on the wooden floor. A group sat together looking at the dim flame of the coopi-lamp.

They all had broken bones. The sun had burned their skins. Some had limbs missing, eyes poked out. I had no doubt it was the place where beggars were beaten into the shape all beggars become. Now I knew why my mother was so fearful of the baby snatchers, warning me never to talk to strangers.

Early Morning, Polished Boots

1.

Two friends playing with marbles
on the dark smooth ground
                under
the soft chin
                of a tall shimul tree
                long beyond its bloom.
                        The sands above them
chewing the tree
                like a caterpillar.

★

They never asked why
                        the sudden thunder
                        of silence
                        wrenched the morning.
Komol's wren-boned body
                        shook
when Omar nominated
                        a cat-eyed marble
for the beat of his strength.

★

But he failed to twang anything,
heard a heavy engine
                humming
  in the ground below
                his bare feet.
Komol's mood slid
  into senseless clay.
A huge military vehicle
                laden with troops
                ammunitions
hurtled along the narrow street.

★

The army pointed
      their heavy guns.
Helmets on the soldiers' heads varnished
   into glazed watermelons.

★

The boys
            were speechless,
                  the morning's
                  sudden nightfall
                        on them.
They heard the vehicle coming
         to a rapid halt
                  the thud of military boots
                  polished with sun-dew
      taking position
                  behind the brick walls.
A hoarse voice vibrating the air
                  asked Komol
                     to give up his mischief
      or a thorny shell from his gun
            would break his body.

★

Komol shed the world,
escaped through the gap in the wall
               where the twisting banyan grew
splitting the sharp grains
            of the brick fence.

★

Omar hid behind the shimul tree.
      Komol fell on the dry ditch
         and ran
behind the banana plants clumped together,
         convinced
he was now safe,
that the army could not see the perfection
               of his husk.

★

Now I am invisible, like the stars in the larkspur sky
                 he thought.
And he could see
       from the thicket of the plantains
the army taking cover behind
         the walls and the tree stems.

★

A bristly moustache
   glistened in the sun.
The soldier nudged a new stanza
   in his rifle's magazine....

★

'Let them wait for the black ducks
       and the great blue heron.
I am going home to my mum,'
   the boy warned.
    The soldier was stroking
       the barrel
   of his automatic.

2.

Komol danced into the house.
His mother sensed trouble:
    'Son, have you just come out
        of a shark's mouth?'
His body swung in powerfully.
  Unable to come up with a story
he sat close to his vanilla-smelling mother
                breast-feeding
                his baby sister.
            He could hear
            the sucking noise
and the sound of his sister's breathing.

                ★

  The wide-eyed child
closed her eyes now and then,
    as if the lids were too heavy.
The windows open
            on the olive-dove
praising the dust that hung
            in the air.

                ★

Komol touched the soft head
of the baby
        felt the fontanel throb
        with the strength of her fast-
growing brain
        as she nested against his mother,
    heard a single crack
                of clear sound
    breaking that moment
into many questions.

★

The house shook
        with the blast,
                sparkling a hole
in the corrugated tin wall.
        Komol heard a noise
                snapping flesh
                and instantly his mother
                slid
                from his arms.

★

His sister's tiny frame lapsed into silence –
        her gum still budding
on his mother's nipple
  not wheezing any more,
though her hand was in her mother's mouth,
taking hold of her last song
to her daughter –
It is all over little one.
Now her other arm
        clutched
  at the abrupt emptiness
  that hung about her brother.

★

Baby's milk poised
        in a rat-coloured hole.
Smoke rose from it like the loveliness
        of thin river-mist.
The reek of burned skin
  wafted through the window into the wood.

Komol felt the drift of blood
                in his feet and hands,
                first warm then cold,
                found himself wet.
Saw his world slip away from him
                like a boat leaving a harbour.
Komol watched his mother's
        convulsions come
                to a sudden sleep
                but he didn't sense
                the length of it or how far
                her soul might have gone,
knew he was no longer in her love
as the summer shadows
                dropped out of the trees.

The Nectarine Tree

Up in the tree the plumpest nectarine,
tight on its stalk, tantalised Rubina.
She couldn't reach it, so with a hazel stick
she tried to knock it loose but it only blushed.

I clopped into sight and offered her
my service, climbed up the twisted trunk,
chose the one which had never been pecked
by ravens or bruised by hailstones.

I twisted the nectarine from its spur
and she spread her skirt like a forbidden flag.
I let it drop straight into the hollow of her cotton.
My heart plopped down with it.

That tree is gone now,
a murderer has built his house on the spot.

Flies

Foes are like flies.
They seek sores
larger and cleaner
than themselves.
Sit on them. Mate.
Rub their legs.
Suck juices out
before laying eggs.
It is in their nature
to poke relentlessly
on raw flesh all day
with their black needles
glimmering like pawpaw seeds.
Nothing pleases them
more than seeing wounds
hung from trees to dry
in the orchid sun.

My Mistress Grounded Me

My mistress grounded me
for killing a tiny rat
and catching a bird
in her back garden.
She lectured me
the whole day long
to make me civilized and human,
said I have to give up
my wild and brutal ways.

She couldn't forget how
the pigeon's grey-white feather
fluttered like a heart
in the cage of my mouth.
How can I tell her
these things come naturally,
just like the aim
of my eye's deft needle?

Since I've been grounded
she hasn't scooped me up on her lap.
I miss her hand on the tips
of my fur, and me
arching my back up
against her hand and purring
for the fiesta of her breast.
In return I'd reach up
and paw her smooth cheek.

My mistress lines the stiff bottom
of a cardboard carton
with a blouse she's worn
so I am singed by her scent.
While she thrashes in her cold sleep,
I scratch at her door till dawn.
The smell of paint climbs
in bracelets toward my face.

MIG-21 Raids at Shegontola

Only this boy moves
between the runes of trees
on his tricycle
when an eagle swoops,
releases two arrows
from its silver wings and melts
away faster than lightning.
Then a loud whistle
and a bang like dry thunder.
In a blink the boy sees
his house roof sink,
feels his ears ripped off.
The blast puffs up a fawn smoke
bigger than a mountain cloud.
The slow begonias rattle
their scarlet like confetti.
Metal slashes
the trees and ricochets.
Wires and pipes snap
at the roots, quiver.
The whirling smoke packed
with bricks and cement,
chicken feathers and nigella seeds.
When the cloud begins
to settle on the ground,
the boy makes out buckled iron rods.
White soot descends
and he finds himself dressed
like an apprentice baker.

Illegitimate

Fatima began her day
as if nothing happened,

though illicit milk
soaked her cotton shirt.

When the wild crows called
she could only think

of her firstborn
no longer in her arms.

The crows hovered
above the town dump

where she'd ditched him, wiped
their claws in the branch

of a bean tree.
She felt her sky going away

in a rush, had to get to her son
before they did

and raced back
but the crows came down on her.

Their horny feet scratched her scalp
until she fell, found herself lying

with fishbones and mouldy bread,
scattered chicken legs.

One voice wrought a black note
as she stood up and ran to him –

saw the crow burst
his lip like a soft seed.

An Open Manhole

The kids needle their way
back to the isomer of water's attraction.

They whirl around the pool's electrons.
They hum as if the rain in them

is nothing next to the rain they're in.
One by one they jump in the iris

of the splash and break the glass.
Below their feet the city drains,

taking the water a long way off to the river
where their fathers and brothers fish.

Come, this rut is deep, says the girl
with a turtle-round face, as she leaps

into the dark centre of the puddle
and immediately is sucked under.

The children gaze into the last ripple
as the lute-eye closes its lid.

Bangladesh

When peasants loot fields through the lotus dusk,
when children collect hailstones on the hush grass,

when ancient trees uproot, reed-roofed houses are blown away
by a wind stronger than Kaytoki's storm-hair,

Bangladesh, the plentiful and destructible, I think of you.

Consider this burden of your famous floods
which hold water-lilies in your bosom year round.

Bangladesh, I'm searching for your homeless –
for where they can set up house in the hearts of mango-people,
fruits exploding on shy branches.

Bangladesh, I'm disappointed in your rice grains thinner than rains
and cattle stouter than cannoniers.

You taught me to swim like your river porpoise, causing my ripples
to crawl out and wet girls' feet on the sands.

Just want to say though how I miss your land. I'm still part
of your root and bud, but my footprint travels less than
        the simplest leaf.

Boy in an Old Photograph

He's holding a split star
in the black holes of his eyes,
unsmiling, gazing out
at the new world:
his small round hands
in the pockets of his shorts,
his dark hair brittle as a shoe-brush,
flat-toed Bata shoes shiny,
socks folded around neat ankles.
He is standing stiff like a pillar
before the rushing stream
of his rolling senses,
muddy meetings of rising waters
in the chaotic city.
Time in slow drops.
His mother is not with him
to lament the humming in the shadows
at the end of his boredom.
Bright light winces off the walls.
No one suspects this picture
will not fit daintily
into the spectrum of his family album.
A pattern is broken.
It is his last photo,
but the camera keeps clicking
every year without him
in the dark lens.

Skylark

This morning I saw a falcon
clawing a skylark in my garden.

I hadn't taught this hawk
to bring down the little birds
from the belladonna sky
with their necks broken.
I couldn't turn my head
but the falcon didn't tear
into the perfect bird that shook
for its life under the talons.

I spoke into the falcon's eyes:
I've better meat for you.
Fly up to me, tear at my wrist
with your savage beak.
Release the lark.
Or fly back to the trainer
who raised you to hunt.
Return to your nest
in the ringing hills.
Bring up a rainbow trout
from the dark water.

The falcon took no notice.
I struck out at the peregrine
with the sharpest of knives
to cut loose the little bird,
but it was carried higher and higher
far beyond the reign of my mind.
I didn't see the skylark fall away
from the falcon's grip –
and my own pride under its claw.

A Basket of Sorrow

A snake charmer came to catch a cobra hiding
inside a water-pot on our rear veranda.

All known miseries strike at his feet when
carefully he rolled the jar over, to force the snake out.

He grabbed it firmly by its tail,
the water-pot didn't turn the way the snake

charmer intended. It rolled with the mouth away
from him, and the snake was gone in a flash,

leaving the mice to roam our yards.
The snake charmer's patience wearing

thin as the clean-smelling cobra's that knew
the strength in his body and the malice of hands.

All that the snake charmer had was his
binagini flute, so he played the note

in that place where tree-wasps dance. The tone
could feel its way between my tongue

and heart – one was too quick and one was
too slow, needing much blood to understand

how the serpent might have been withered by his scorn,
for this cunning cobra had now gone back

to its lair under the bamboo bush. The snake
twitched in the hedge, knew the man

was looking to smash its nest.
His spade was a gleam going into the ground

with a beat not quite matching the reptile's,
now chiselling away the earth little by little.

And the snake hid under its own coil
where every scale shone grief.

Bidisha on the Wall

Her picture on the west wall
makes it hard to forget
how special Bidisha was.
I feel like breaking every mirror
in the house, as she sits thoughtfully
on the edge of a balloon-back chair.
This woman is not coming down to me
from the cold wall into my warm bed.
It is tough to look at her
without recalling the incident
that pulled her boat towards the heavy mouth
of the long furtive river of the fish-valley.
I have no idea how she let go the hands
of the one she danced with until the ship capsized.
All I know is that she was in that disco boat
catching the morphine moons
in her glasses of champagne,
over the cold-tongued, thousand-eyed Thames.

Mind of a Stone

I am a nameless stone, sitting by the sea-voice,
tearing silence from the noises of the underworld.

From the light's lake I steal the brightest minds
and lock them in my body. I want them

to brush my life with leaf shadows.
My blood is hotter than the sun's sperm.

Why do you want to see through me? Nothing is going to
                                                    slip out
of me. Even if you call I will not hear you.

I will not bend towards you even if you are homeless.
If you wish to know the herbs of pain you can pound

your body against mine but nothing will happen.
I am breathless. I am made of shock and speechlessness.

Tragedy is my trade. Grief will not stop the buttercups growing
in the battlefield. Hone your knives. Heat me up for a battle.

A Lizard by My Hospital Bed

The mouth of silence trickles forward a bloodless lizard.
I take off my oxygen mask and allow

his cracked sound to crawl into my teenage head.
Like me he puffs for air. I wheeze. He pants.

He does not break his meditation as the hours pass,
my eyes still on him when he jumps on a thinking fly

with a fine open-air gesture. An education by lizard:
focus, don't rely on impulse.

Keep the foam clear so my voice doesn't burst
through my trachea hole

like shrapnel in a pomegranate.
My eyes flick a question, city kerosene-thuds

echoing in my head. My friend says nothing.
Goes one step back, two steps forward.

How can I let him go? I grab the fellow by his tail,
but he still escapes through the gap in my throat.

Bullet

A bullet sheared my voice away before I could flee
and I have been bargaining with him ever since
as if he was a relative planning a long stay.
He has reason to come because I was a troublemaker,

a vermin, smelled of subversive acts against the state,
if I opened my mouth the weather changed faster
than language in heat. Revolt is the first literature.
He has a country to run. He uses songs to slay the enemy.

If I do not sing the venom into people I will come out
mangled, he warned. Now he sits like a thorn between
my vocal chords, dictating how my tongue should dance
to those chants. But they mean nothing to me.

What dwells in my throat are words, heavy like imperfect stones
rattling to express the emptiness of my mouth, wanting
to speak, wanting to explain that I will stop painting the city
with fire in exchange for a fragment of my voice.

He has been living with me for such a long time that sometimes
I want my heart to beat like him. Maybe I trust him,
I am not kidding. My son needs an uncle. He can stay
as long as he does not land at my feet like a grenade.

My Maestro

We slow down to see the bones
beneath this sweet maestro's song –
we wish we had his formula
to open the world for you just as he did for us.

Everything nearby turns tender:
Cheetahs stop running after deer,
hornets hover over the flowers' ports
and travellers anchor in the bay.

This is how he speaks to our tuneless blood
to savour the notes of breaking stones,
laying a road inside us so we find ourselves –
who we really are and what we become.

The next time you walk this way, think
of this house on the narrow road across country
and of the maestro who plays his guitar
and of how the rain's rhythm sounds right.

He won't run off with everything you have.
The maestro's thinking of you. He knows
what keeps your family together, how you swim
through life when you feel heavy and small.

If you push out anywhere towards the sea
once the percale of your bed vanishes,
he won't let you drift away so easily.
Such is the strength of his music.

Dog Seed

A nine-year-old scrambles out of his tin shack
to find two dogs jammed rump to rump –
a gruff mongrel with slashing jaws
dragging another up the street, a third of its size,
yowling at the grip of the knot, from which
it can't run. As the sun fries the fleas on their backs,
the boy decides to pull them apart.

So with a rogue stick he whacks the stud.
Then quick as a shuttle their frightened bodies
crash into the guy rope tethered to the ground,
tearing them from their filaments, her sex
bulbous as an injured strawberry, the inner skin
inside out, its pulp glinting between taut thighs.

The sire's virgule is an imperfect scarlet lipstick
half severed – looks as if it's been chewed.
Something milky, like gum seeds, comes out
of the gangling rod and daubs the tarmac,
its heat-odour calling to flies and ants,
the air heady with the ragged smell of release.

When Bangladesh Floats
in a Water-hyacinth

I will visit you
when my country floats
in a water-hyacinth,
and ponder how much
I know of your flavour
by catching boaal
and chital fish together.

I will walk the sunset
that loses itself
in your plum-black water.
I have come to admire
the resilience of this tiger land
where the snake takes on a life
quicker than my hands,

adding its signature
branch by branch,
then surprises me
when the floodwater returns
over and over to trace
the same monsoon tide.
Rice grasses rustle

as I row my pleasure boat over
their smallest leaning
and it is time, once again
to get to know
the clay at the river-bottom
that colours my skin
like comforting chocolate.

My Aim Now is to
Waste Time Luxuriously

When I live a life in deferment
light doesn't fall on my garden.
Spring delays its colourful delivery.
Squirrels stay away until summer.
I am in no hurry to leave my house.
My habits don't leave their dens
until the moment the rope coils around
my neck and I pull like an archer.

Think of all the time I've wasted,
never have I been so fallen as today.
I've been a cheat and must put a stop
to it without dithering or bickering.
Less sleep more work, this is how
I now set my life to serve me best.
Today my heart is a beggar, begging
to let me go. The only healthy thing
to do is to walk away from my lazy body,
so the little time I've to live is decent.

Suzanne

Suzanne must sit before her mirror every morning
to gather the woman at the roots of her hair.

She colours herself as if all her lush has gone.
All her grief is in her make-up.

She belongs to the Tormentil plant.
She is made of four petals: vain and vulnerable, delicate
    and discreet.

Before breakfast she has to powder her face with
    sun-crushed flowers,
with her cinnamon-umber lipstick

or the coral she wears to match the tone of her startled skin.
The early sun needles slantwise through the window,

prickling the dance of atom-seeds in the room,
her fluent neck entirely gold, glinting with intention.

Her eyelids flutter like Jackanapes.
She is never careless with her face. She knows what
    goes where

and how much to put on.·
Sweet smell of her talcum, musky eyelashes carry the uprising

of elderberry to the syllable of her blood.
When she is at the dressing table her face is never dark

with the monologue of a city's gasoline.
Who will dare to send rain to wash it all away now?

Why Doesn't My Sister Sing to Me Anymore?

My sister woke early
to catch the mist
in her flower basket.
She arranged the zinnias,
asters, prongs of phlox.
Shall I wake him,
I could hear her think,
take him out of sleep
and roll him in the apple grass?

She cleared her throat
and started a familiar hymn,
All joy is in the dark
vessels of the skin!
She held me in her melody,
letting the music suck
into the mountains,
the northern waves.
I swear I lost the beast in me.

To Have My Sister Back

Deeba, did you know
I went to your room yesterday
looking for you?
The room was so dark
I thought you were sleeping.
I tiptoed, whispered your name
in a hanged-man's voice
 – Deeba – Deeba – Deeba.
I drew the curtains
to catch your eyes in the light.

You were not there
only everything else that was yours:
saris in the alna,
lipstick, hair clips, hairbrush
on the dressing table,
finger marks on the mirror,
tablas on the almira,
tanpura and sitar leaning
on the side of your bed.

It looked as though
nothing visits your room
but the pungent soil
of the growing city
trying to claim
hold of your belongings.

An overpowering silence in the room,
so strong that I could
hear your invisible hands
still tapping the tablas,

so I picked up the tanpura
and pulled its string
to bring back
a little melody
to the room
that died with you.

She May be in the Summer Berries

Suppose you trap the only smile
your sister left for you

in the room of your memory.
Or ask the cloud-rivers

why she disappeared. The answer
may be in the names of summer berries.

Maybe you become something
bigger than the berries

in their final shaking. And you
become a seed homesick for growth

so a laugh can burst from the earth.

Famine

Last night, the full moon hung like a thin chapatti
before my hungry mouth.

My Father, a Disconnected Man

Nobody wastes worry on this near-blind old man,
who is nearly weightless, sheathed in rumpled clothes.
He dried up like a low-slung fish.
Nothing lifts his blood. Probably that is why
he talks little, answers no call.
From the silkiness of the morning wind he weaves
a tree's silence to the gate of first light.
It is hard to tell whether he still exists.
He is aware the world is rotating without him,
and seeks a way of breathing in this climate.
At mealtimes his wife summons him to eat,
but after dinner his entire family swiftly vanishes
into the front room to watch television.
He hears the clock's hands slow to fill his day
and puffs discreetly on a Dunhill.
The ruined light of an unspoken candle keeps him calm.
The river wind riffles his thistle-frost hair
as if it is in the room asking him to fold up
all light like a blanket and step out
of the door that kept him out of the rain.
As if it is the address where he can call back
his loved ones into his body at will.

Still Birth

After so many miscarriages
this bone-shine baby
with its heart pounding
like a moondark dawn
with a promise of black hair and teak eyes
and a little more than one foot long.
As she lay on the silver tray
I could see where she'd have her dimple
and how it'd pull me into the whorl
that'd catch my breath.
For a moment I forgot
she had no river-buds in her pulse
and no zit of lights in her eyes.
Yet it seemed she laughed.
I picked up my girl gently,
her marble head tipped back
in the cup of my hot hand.
Her arms didn't spread
into the wings of a seagull.
I let her float in the room's sky
as I shook her in my hands.
Then I wrapped up her tiny body
in swaddling cloth
and put her in a Jones shoe box.

Mother to Son

Playing with my doll was a dress rehearsal –
it refined the green rain of my contentment.
For you I perfumed my skin with mush petal,

felt a seed looked the same as a comet-tail,
tapped the pathway of my heaven's gate,
fearing once you were in my tummy

I'd shut you in there forever. Then I thought
you wouldn't fit in my body, where you swim
in the pink water with your tiny blown shadow.

I fed you my blood like hibiscus sucking
the slow heat rising from the soil.
Slowly, you blossomed.

My waters burst first, then I pushed you hard.
You slid out of my body on the thousandth breath –
slippery and shiny with birth juice.

You clamped onto me. My first milk foamed.
Your freshness hovered over my sky
like the voice of a tulip.

Your foal eyes shone through the window of my blood.
Immediately, I took your hand in my mouth,
sucked it in time with you.

My Child, Cycling

Not so long ago he was scared
of his own soft shadow
as if it dug his grave.
He demanded I stay with him
to guard his camp and protect
the ground from sinking.

Now he knows how to ride
along the roads without my eyes
pulling the tail of his shirt,
stopping him making sparks.
I stay speechless while he chants:

I must go ahead and praise the sun.
Your city is hungry and airless.
I want to free myself from dirt
and embrace the rhythm of pure air.
But, I will not betray your spirit.
Freeing himself from my arms,
he rides ahead.

Even though he is aware it's bad luck
he turns to look at me.
My sight is weak but I can see
what he hides in the depth of his heart.
I watch him vanishing uphill towards
the air over the tree line,
where an orange globe
opens like a flower.

I Want to Change the Course of a Great River

I was terribly shaken this morning when I came out of my house
and saw the sun's radiant light touching your nipples and lips.

I scrambled to your waterfall where I felt the round nakedness
of your two great heights – I knelt at your pool and took

the rushing droplets on my tongue for body's sudden joy.
Drinking from such a powerful flowing source, I want to change

the way it rolls past my rain-chilled natal hamlet for good. Then
at once I will build a grasshut with the sharp fragments of my past.

An English Viper and Indian Cobra

The English viper in my mouth lost its tongue.
Once it could swell up in anger,
let off a hiss as it deflated.
I fed it rats to ensure
it would produce high quality venom
and guard me against fatal diseases.

Perhaps it needs a cobra as a mate
so I search for one in the swamps of India
to catch one by its tail and carry it
like a black skipping-rope in a calico bag.

I show it to the viper in my mouth.
The dorsal scales look black, clean,
delicate, but the muzzle and throat
are pale as ivory, and the spread hood
makes the shoulder look like a sitting hawk.
The face is startlingly bird-like, accipitrine,
flat-headed, the eye bright as polished jet.

When I move closer it suddenly spits
and throws its head – glimpse
of pink mouth opens to the gullet –
and I find my trousers wet with venom.
It turns on my right hand,
strikes repeatedly downwards,
like a seabird breaking a shell on a stone.

I put the cobra with the viper in my mouth.
In no time the two coil together
and begin to whisper in two different tongues,
rubbing each other's slender bodies.
A bright orange fluid sprays out
and fills my mouth like liquid pollen,
inoffensive, with a faint
spicy smell of curry powder.

My Son Waits by the Door

We live on a council estate, my son and I.
Nine years old, but he looks much younger.
He has not yet learnt to read the minds

and motives of our neighbours. It's a month
now since they stopped playing with him:
Heather, Helen, Edmond and Simon.

When I bring him home from school he
doesn't take off his jacket, but waits.
When a breeze whistles past the house

he opens the blue door with a smile
to see whether anybody stands outside
asking him to play on the reckless street

with its smut; but no-one is there.
A long emptiness howls like a hyena –
his path is now slippery with its saliva.

Weathered by what happened
he stares past the neighbourhood
and makes his way back into the house.

The Last Apple in a Bowl of Fruit

Every time I come to the kitchen
you invite me to bite into you
and eat the pulp of your existence.

How do you feel when I arrange
other fruits delicately in this bowl,
belly to belly and skin to skin?

The vulgar readiness of bananas,
the papayas swollen with brief pink milk,
and passion fruits ripe with remembering.

My intention is to consume you
when I'm totally empty of tenderness
and my tongue is wickedly restless.

I'll let the waiting sudden juice
arrive slowly in my eager mouth
and onto my caressing hands.

I want to break open a new life
and discover your last impulses,
until I reach the seeds at your core.

Acknowledgements

Acknowledgements are due to the editors of the following publications in which some of these poems first appeared: *Ambit, London Magazine, PN Review, Poetry* (Chicago)*, Poetry Review, Poetry London, Ten: New Poets from Spread the Word* editors Bernardine Evaristo and Daljit Nagra (Bloodaxe, 2010).

'My Salma', 'Early Morning, Polished Boots', 'To Have My Sister Back', were shortlisted for the 2007 New Writing Ventures Awards.

Grateful thanks to Arts Council England for a Grant for the Arts award, to enable me to finish this manuscript.

With grateful thanks to Pascale Petit, Moniza Alvi, Sarah Snell, Nathalie Teitler, Jennifer Langer, James Dawson, Mir Mahmud Ali Plato, Selina K. Mir and Kinshuk Mir for their friendship, advice and encouragement through many difficult times.

About the Author

Mir Mahfuz Ali was born in Dhaka, Bangladesh. He studied at Essex University. He dances, acts, has worked as a male model and a tandoori chef. As a performer, he is renowned for his extraordinary voice – a rich, throaty whisper brought about by a Bangladeshi policeman trying to silence the singing of anthems during a public anti-war demonstration. He has given readings and performances at Royal Opera House, Covent Garden and other theatres in Britain and beyond.